ANIMAL STORY

ORANGUTAN RESCUE

by Dougal Dixon

With thanks to our consultant, Dr. Gary Shapiro, Ph.D. Vice President, Orangutan Foundation International

WATERBIRD BOOKS

Columbus, Ohio

ANIMAL STORY

ORANGUTAN RESCUE

 Children's Publishing

This edition published in the United States of America in 2004 by
Waterbird Books
an imprint of McGraw-Hill Children's Publishing,
a Division of The McGraw-Hill Companies
8787 Orion Place
Columbus, Ohio 43240-4027

www.MHkids.com

Library of Congress Cataloging-in-Publication Data is on file with the publisher.

First published in Great Britain in 2004 by *ticktock* Media Ltd.,
Unit 2 Orchard Business Centre, North Farm Road, Tunbridge Wells, Kent TN3 3XF.
Text and illustrations © 2004 *ticktock* Entertainment Ltd.
We would like to thank: Lorna Cowan, Jean Coppendale and Elizabeth Wiggans.
Every effort has been made to trace the copyright holders, and we apologize in advance for any unintentional omissions.
We would be pleased to insert the appropriate acknowledgements in any subsequent edition of this publication.

All rights reserved. Except as permitted under the United States Copyright Act, no part of this publication may be reproduced or distributed in any form or by any means, or stored in a database retrieval system, without prior written permission from the publisher.

Printed in China

1-57768-898-8

1 2 3 4 5 6 7 8 9 10 TTM 09 08 07 06 05 04

The *McGraw·Hill* Companies

CONTENTS

CHANG, THE BABY ORANGUTAN — 4
Foraging for food — 6

LIFE IN THE RAIN FOREST — 8
Meet Chang's father — 10

RAIN FOREST IN DANGER — 12
Poachers in the forest — 14

ORANGUTAN FOR SALE — 16
A tiny prisoner — 18

A DARING ESCAPE — 20
At the rehabilitation center — 22

ORANGUTAN RESCUE — 24
Learning to be an orangutan — 26

ORANGUTAN FACT FILE — 28

GLOSSARY — 31

INDEX — 32

CHANG, THE BABY ORANGUTAN

It is warm. The air is moist. There is plenty of food. Chang is a baby orangutan. He is two years old.

As soon as he was born, Chang held onto the fur on his mother's chest. He will continue to cling to her until he is about three years old.

For the first few months of his life, Chang fed on only his mother's milk. As he grew, his mother began to feed him fruit that she had chewed into a pulp.

Now, he is older. Chang is able to find food for himself. He still drinks his mother's milk and will continue to do so until he is about five years old.

Chang will stay with his mother until he is about seven years old. During Chang's early years, his mother will teach him how to care for himself.

Chang and his mother live high in the treetops of the Borneo rain forest in southeast Asia. Above them, the sky is hidden by green foliage. Beneath them, a dense tangle of trees and plants grows.

The forest canopy supplies all of their food. Orangutans eat mainly fruit, such as figs and a coconut-sized fruit covered in spines, called *durian*. They also eat leaves and bark. Birds' eggs, snails, ants, and termites supply orangutans with protein.

Sitting in a tree, Chang's mother eats a durian fruit. Using her hands, Chang's mother throws away the skin and seeds. Then, she shares the sweet flesh with Chang. When they have eaten their fruit, the two orangutans move on. Nearby, a monkey climbs up the tree. He is also looking for food.

With Chang clinging to her, Chang's mother walks across a broad, horizontal branch to another tree. She grasps an overhead branch and then swings to another tree. This acrobatic way of moving is called *brachiating*. Orangutans cross the forest using this method.

LIFE IN THE RAIN FOREST

It is getting late. Soon it will be night. It is time for Chang's mother to build a nest.

She bends branches and wedges them into the fork of a tree trunk. She weaves them together so they are stiff. Chang's mother does this until she has built a bowl-shaped platform. Then, she collects leaves that she will use to line the nest, making the nest soft and warm.

Above the canopy of trees, the moon rises in the sky. Only a little of its light penetrates the dense forest. The daytime animals, such as tree-living lizards and snakes, have disappeared. The nocturnal (nighttime) animals, such as lorises and tarsiers, begin to stir. In the distance, crocodiles splash in the moonlit water. A monkey crosses the swamp.

It starts to rain. Chang's mother pulls a large leaf over the nest to keep them dry. Then, the two orangutans settle down for the night.

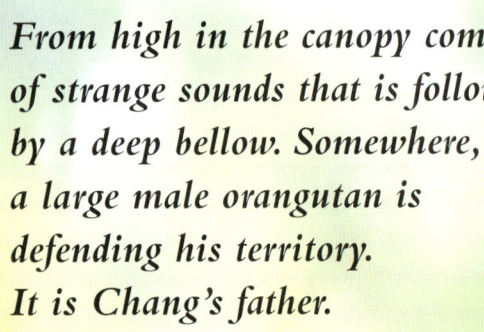

From high in the canopy comes a series of strange sounds that is followed by a deep bellow. Somewhere, a large male orangutan is defending his territory. It is Chang's father.

Unlike other primates, adult orangutans live alone. They gather together only to mate. Occasionally, two or more males fight and wrestle over their territory. In his short life, Chang has seen only one orangutan, his mother. Chang's father has never been around him.

A male orangutan is nearly twice the size of a female. He has a long, shaggy coat of red hair. Like all orangutans, he is tree-dwelling, or *arboreal*.

Even though large cats, such as tigers and clouded leopards, are rare in these forests, orangutans climb high in the trees to avoid them. Their instinct tells them to fear these animals.

Chang's father has large, soft, leatherlike cheek pads and a hanging pouch of skin at his throat. Researchers believe these features make him look big and fierce when he challenges other males. These features also help him to make his booming call. When trying to attract females, his large cheek pads show that he is mature, healthy, and will make a good mate.

RAIN FOREST IN DANGER

The forest seems safe to Chang and his mother. The orangutans do not understand that their home is in danger.

This is southeast Asia, one of the most crowded places on earth. As the human population grows, people need farmland to grow food. They cut down the rain forests to farm.

Others see the rain forest as an opportunity to make money. People chop down trees and sell the wood. They do not realize that, without the trees, the forest animals will have no place to live. Governments around the world try to protect the rain forests. They pass laws that govern the amount and kind of logging that can take place. But many companies break these laws.

As the forests shrink, animals have a harder time finding food. The orangutans are forced to live closer and closer together.

Loss of habitat is not the only threat that the orangutans face. People, called *poachers*, illegally take orangutans from their habitat and sell them. Poachers sell young apes for large sums of money to people wanting them for pets.

Chang and his mother awaken as the misty light of dawn filters through the forest canopy. There are strange noises coming from far below. People are hacking away at the trees.

The loggers and poachers have seen the orangutan nest. They have spotted the mother and baby inside. Now, they are cutting down all of the surrounding trees. Chang's mother will not be able to escape by swinging from branch to branch. Eventually, hunger will bring her down to the ground.

The poachers do not have to wait long. Seeing no other way to escape, Chang's mother starts to climb down the tree trunk.

Then, the poachers strike. They pull her from the tree. It is only the baby they want. Chang is torn from his mother's arms. Laughing and shouting, the overjoyed poachers carry off their prize. Chang will never see his mother again.

ORANGUTAN FOR SALE

The world has changed for Chang. The poachers have taken him from the forest and from his mother.

Chang is now surrounded by strange, new smells and noises. Huge dogs growl at him through the bars of his cage. Chang is for sale in a busy market. There is a lot of shouting and bargaining going on around him. Someone has decided to buy Chang.

Chang's new home is a cage, in a luxury apartment. The poachers sold Chang to a family that lives in a big city far from where he was born.

Chang has toys to play with, but they are nothing like the twigs and insects he played with in the forest. His new family feeds him, but the food makes him sick. He lives on a diet of soda, potato chips, and cookies. He is let out of the cage to play only when his owners want to show him to their friends.

Some days, he lies curled up in a corner of his cage. He wraps his arms around his body, hugging himself. In the forest, his mother was always there to hug him. His young owners are annoyed that he is so inactive. Now, they ignore him most of the time.

Today, as the family leaves the apartment, they throw some food into Chang's cage. They are very careless and they do not close his cage door properly.

Chang thumps the bars and the door swings open. He is free.

A DARING ESCAPE

Now, Chang has a chance to explore the apartment. He soon finds some interesting treasures.

He does not know what the items are, but he plays with them anyway. Like a little tornado, he whirls around his young owner's bedroom, leaving a mess behind.

Clambering around the bathroom, Chang accidentally turns on the faucet. He takes a drink of water. In the forest, Chang lapped water from leaves and licked rain from his mother's fur.

An exciting new world lies beyond an open window. There is a jungle of tall apartment buildings and office blocks. Chang clambers down the fire escape and scampers between the legs of surprised people in the street. Cars and bicycles swerve past him. People shout as they crash into one another.

As night falls, Chang grows tired. He tries to rest in a filthy alleyway. Suddenly, Chang hears voices. Lights flash in his eyes, and then all is dark. Someone throws a blanket over him, and he is captive once more.

Chang is on a long, white table. He is surrounded by people. He is not aware though, because he has been drugged.

For the first time in his life, Chang is surrounded by people who are concerned about his well-being. The people who captured him in the city work for an organization dedicated to stopping the illegal trade of orangutans. Now, they have brought Chang back to Borneo. He is in the examination room of an orangutan rehabilitation center.

The veterinarians at the center are examining Chang. Captive orangutans can catch human diseases. The veterinarians take blood samples from Chang to check for diseases, such as tuberculosis and hepatitis. Then, they fingerprint Chang and put a tiny identification chip under his skin.

Next, Chang will be put in an isolated area for three weeks because he may have been infected with some other disease that the examination missed. During this time in quarantine, veterinarians will give him medical care and special attention.

After his time in quarantine, the veterinarians will introduce Chang to other orangutans at the center.

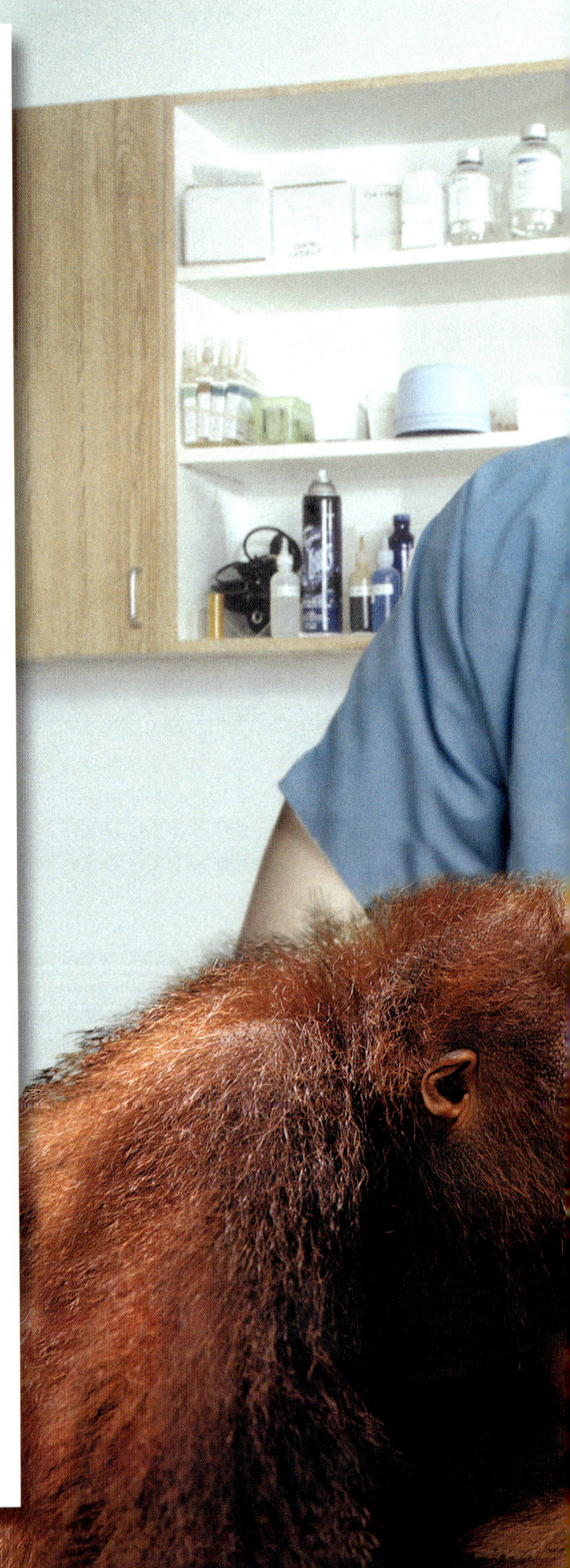

ORANGUTAN RESCUE

Chang is back in a cage, but this cage is so big that he does not even realize where he is. Branches and leaves surround him, and he can see the forest.

Now, Chang is in a colony with several other young orangutans of the same age. All of them have been taken from private homes, poorly-run roadside zoos, or pet dealers. The orangutans are about to begin their training for a return to the wild.

Each day, the caretakers take the young orangutans into the trees. They encourage the animals to climb and move around in the branches. The caretakers give the young orangutans milk. They place fruit and vegetables high on a feeding platform to encourage the animals to climb. Like young children, orangutans have to be taught about their environment and how to care for themselves.

It is warm. The air is moist. There is plenty of food. It is five years later, and Chang is back in the forest.

All the orangutans in Chang's group at the rehabilitation center are nearly adults. In the wild, they would have learned life skills from their mothers in their first five years. Their mothers would have taught them how to climb, how to swing, how to gather fruit, and how to build nests. The rescued orangutans have had to learn survival techniques from their human handlers and from each other.

Now, the orangutans' caretakers are setting them free into an area of protected rain forest. It is not the complete freedom that the orangutans would have known in the wild. The scientists will check on Chang and the other orangutans all the time.

For every rescued orangutan like Chang, many other baby orangutans and their mothers die at the hands of poachers. As each year goes by, huge areas of the orangutans' habitat disappear.

In just ten years, orangutans could no longer exist, or become *extinct,* in the wild. Chang and many other animals need all the protection we can give them.

ORANGUTAN FACT FILE

The name *orangutan* means "person of the forest" in the Malay language. The orangutan has also been called the "old man of the woods." The orangutan's scientific name is *Pongo pygmaeus*. The words come from *mpongi*, an African word for "ape." They also come from the word *pygmy*, meaning "small."

THE WORLD OF THE ORANGUTAN

Wild orangutans are found only in tropical rain forests on the islands of Borneo and Sumatra in southeast Asia.

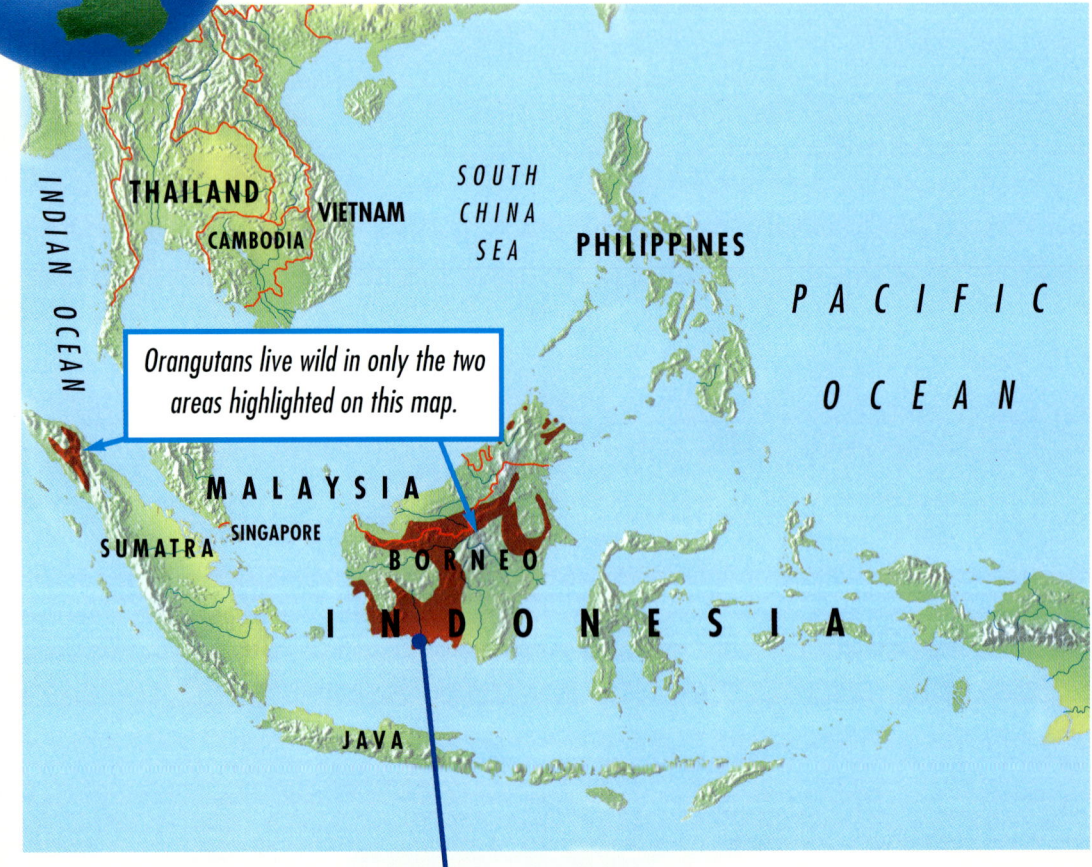

Orangutans live wild in only the two areas highlighted on this map.

TANJUNG PUTING NATIONAL PARK

This park is one of the largest protected areas in southeast Asia. The park includes 1,173 square miles of wild and natural swamps and rain forests. Nearly 6,000 orangutans live there.

- Other primates living in the park include lorises, tarsiers, one species of gibbon, and five different species of monkey. Other creatures in the park include clouded leopards, civets, Malaysian sun bears, and flying fox bats.
- There are over 220 species of birds living in the park. Over 600 species of trees and 200 species of orchid also grow there.

PHYSICAL CHARACTERISTICS

FEMALE

Height: 2.6—3.5 feet tall
Average weight: 110 pounds

MALE

Height: 3.2—4.5 feet tall
Average weight: 200 pounds

- The orangutan is the largest tree-living animal in the world.
- In captivity, orangutans can live to be 50 years old.
- Fully-grown, adult, male orangutans have large, soft, leatherlike cheek pads, and a pouch of skin that hangs at their throats. Researchers believe that these features show females that the male is mature and healthy. These features also help the male to make his territorial and mating calls.
- Large male orangutans can have arms that span up to 7.5 feet, which is the width of a large car!

DIET

- Orangutans eat over 400 different kinds of food.
- The orangutan's main diet is fruit, such as figs and durian fruit (a coconut-sized fruit with a spiny skin and sweet, cheesy-flavored flesh). The orangutan will also eat leaves and bark.
- For protein, orangutans will eat birds' eggs, snails, ants, and termites.

REPRODUCTION AND YOUNG

- Orangutans weigh less than 4 pounds when they are born. That is about the same weight as a large bag of sugar.
- Young orangutans drink their mothers' milk until they are about five years old.
- Mother orangutans chew up fruit for their babies to eat.
- Mother orangutans carry their babies until their young are about three years old.
- Orangutans stay with their mothers until they are about seven years old.
- Unlike other large primates (gorillas and chimpanzees), orangutan mothers have to teach their babies everything without the help of a group.
- A wild female orangutan will have two or three babies in her lifetime.

BEHAVIOR AND SENSES

- Orangutans use their hands and feet to hold things. Like human beings, they have opposable thumbs (a thumb that can be bent around to meet the other fingers). They also have opposable big toes on their feet!
- Male orangutans sometimes make calls and bellows that can carry for over a mile!
- Orangutans use leaves to scoop up water, to shelter themselves from rain, to handle spiny fruit, and to wipe their chins!
- Orangutans live high in the forest canopy—98 feet above the forest floor. This is about eight or nine stories up.
- At night, orangutans build nests of branches and leaves in which to sleep.
- Adult orangutans live alone, coming together only to mate. Occasionally, if there is a good crop of fruit in one tree, several orangutans may gather in the same place. While they feed, the orangutans completely ignore each other, though. On rare occasions, large males will battle with each other to claim a territory.

CONSERVATION

There are only about 20,000 to 25,000 orangutans left living in the rain forest. In just ten years, orangutans could be extinct in the wild.

HABITAT LOSS

- In the last 20 years, 80 percent of the orangutan's forest habitat has been destroyed.
- Rain forest trees are cut down for timber. They are also cut down to be made into paper. Most logging that occurs is illegal.
- Areas of rain forest are cleared for farms, for palm oil plantations, and for gold mining.
- Some farmers will kill orangutans that have strayed onto their farms. They are considered pests!
- When too many orangutans are forced to live in small areas of forest, food becomes difficult to find. If a forest fire occurs in that area, many more orangutans will die.

THE ILLEGAL PET TRADE AND POACHING

- Poachers kidnap baby orangutans from the forest then sell them in markets in Malaysia and Indonesia.
- Every mother orangutan that is killed during the capture of her baby is one less reproductive female living in the forest.
- Most baby orangutans kidnapped from the forest for the pet trade do not survive. Out of every ten captured, about eight or nine die!
- Orangutans are often taken from roadside zoos. These zoos are sometimes set-up to attract people to a nearby shop or other attraction. The animals live in small, dirty cages without adequate food or shelter.

HELPING THE ORANGUTANS

- When orangutans are rescued from illegal pet traders, they are taken to care and quarantine centers. There, veterinarians check them and then put them in quarantine to ensure that they are not passing diseases on to the other apes at the center.

In rehabilitation centers, human caretakers and older, more experienced orangutans reteach young orangutans how to climb, how to swing, how to gather fruit, and how to build nests. When the orangutans are ready, they go to live in areas of forest that are protected by law from poaching and logging. There are rehabilitation centers in Borneo and Sumatra.

WHAT CAN I DO TO HELP?

- Buy only recycled paper.
- Make sure that any wooden items your family buys (such as shelves, wooden flooring, and pool cues) have the FSC label (Forest Stewardship Council). This means the wood comes from a sustainable source (wood that can be regrown quickly).
- Join an organization like the "Orangutan Foundation International." These organizations raise funds to help rescued orangutans. They also work to protect the rain forest: *www.orangutan.org*
- Raise awareness! Tell everyone you know about orangutans and show them this list of things that they can do to help.

GLOSSARY

ARBOREAL Describes animals that live in trees.

BRACHIATING Swinging from branch to branch using the arms.

CANOPY The area of a forest located 130 feet (or about 11 stories) about the ground. This layer receives the most sunshine, allowing leaves, flowers, and fruit to grow there. Most of the forest wildlife is found in the canopy.

HEPATITIS A serious blood disease (normally affecting human beings) that causes the liver to become inflamed.

HOME RANGE The area in which an animal will live over the course of many months or years.

INSTINCT An animal's natural response to the surrounding environment.

LORIS A small, tree-dwelling, nocturnal primate that has thick fur and dark patches around its eyes. It eats insects and lizards.

NOCTURNAL Describes an animal that is active only at night.

NUTRITIOUS Having a large amount of vitamins, minerals, or other nutrients that an animal or human being needs in order to grow and be healthy.

POACHERS People who kill animals illegally or take them from their natural habitat.

PRIMATES An animal group that includes monkeys, apes, and prosimians (animals such as tarsiers and lorises).

PULP A mass of something that is soft and wet.

RAIN FOREST A thick evergreen forest that is located in tropical areas where there is heavy rainfall. The rain forest is organized in layers.

REHABILITATION CENTER A facility that cares for wild animals and prepares them to be returned to the wild.

TARSIER A small, furry, tree-dwelling, nocturnal primate that has a long tail, huge eyes, and good hearing. It eat insects.

TERRITORY The area that one animal defends against other animals to keep its food supply, its family, and its mates safe.

TROPICAL Describes places near the equator that are hot and receive a lot of rain.

TUBERCULOSIS An infectious disease (normally affecting human beings). The victim suffers a high fever and is covered with lumps throughout his or her body, especially in the lungs.

QUARANTINE Describes a period of time that an animal or person spends away from other animals to ensure that it is not carrying any infectious diseases.

INDEX

A
ants 6, 29
arboreal animals 10, 31

B
babies/young 5, 25, 29
behavior 29
birds 8, 28
birds' eggs 6, 29
Borneo 6, 22, 28, 30
brachiating 7, 31

C
canopy 6, 8, 29, 31
cheek pads 11, 29
civets 28
clouded leopards 10, 28
colony 25
confiscated 25, 30, 31
conservation 30
crocodiles 8, 10

D
diseases 22, 30
drink 20
durian fruit 6, 29

F
farming 12, 30
feet 29
figs 6, 29
flying fox bats 28
food 5, 6, 18, 25, 29
Forest Stewardship Council (FSC) 30
fruit 6, 29

G
gibbons 28
gold mining 30

H
habitat 6, 12, 13, 26, 28, 30
hands 6, 29
hepatitis 22, 31
human beings 12, 14, 22, 30

I
insects 8

L
learning 5, 25, 26, 29, 30
leopards 10, 28
lizards 8
logging 12, 14, 30
logging, laws against 12, 30
lorises 8, 28, 31

M
Malaysian sun bears 28
markets 16, 30
mating 10, 11
   see also reproduction
monkeys 6, 8, 28

N
nests 8, 26, 29
nocturnal animals 8, 31
nutrition 5, 31

O
orangutan, female 5, 29
orangutan, male 10, 11, 29
orangutan, scientific name 28
orchids 28

P
palm oil plantations 30
pet trade 16, 30
poachers 13, 14, 26, 30, 31
Pongo pygmaeus 28
primates 10, 28, 31

Q
quarantine 22, 30, 31

R
rain forest 6, 8, 12, 28, 31
rehabilitation 22, 25, 26, 30, 31
reproduction 29
   see also mating

S
size 29
snails 6, 29
snakes 8, 10
status symbol 13, 31

Sumatra 28, 30

T
Tanjung Puting National Park 28
tarsiers 8, 28, 31
teaching 5, 25, 29, 30
termites 6, 29
territory 10, 29, 31
tigers 10
timber/wood 12, 30
toys 18
trees 12, 28, 31
   see also canopy
tuberculosis 22, 31

W
weight 10, 29
wood/timber 12, 30

Y
young/babies 5, 25, 26, 29

PICTURE CREDITS

t=top, b=bottom, c=center, l=left, r=right, OFC=outside front cover, OBC=outside back cover

Alamy: 6c, 6-7c, 9t, 12-13, 15, 16c, 16-17 (main), 18-19 (background), 20t, 21, 24-25. Corbis: 10-11, 22-23 (background). Digital Vision: OFC, 1c, 4-5, 7c, 9br, 12c, 14t, 14b, 20b, 21br, 26-27, 28, 29, 30, 31, OBC. Photodisc: 18-19c.

Every effort has been made to trace the copyright holders, and we apologize in advance for any unintentional omissions. We would be pleased to insert the appropriate acknowledgements in any subsequent edition of this publication.

Printed in the USA
CPSIA information can be obtained
at www.ICGtesting.com
CBHW081446010924
13781CB00055B/690

It wasn't until the 4th Century B.C. that Yu Xi, the Chinese scholar argued that the earth was not resting on anything. Once again the Biblical text proceeds the discovery (or hypothesis) by hundreds of years.

How could men have known these things about the universe before science discovered them? I believe the apostle Peter explains this:

"Knowing this first, that no prophecy of the scripture is of any private interpretation. For the prophecy came not in old time by the will of man: but men of God spake as they were moved by the Holy Ghost."
–2 Peter 1:20-21

On the macroscopic scale

We see symmetry and order in the world all around us, from hexagons in beehives and beneath glacier ice, to manifestations in nature of the Mandelbrot set and Fibonacci sequence.

On the atomic and subatomic scales

The fact that atoms can be arranged into the Periodic Table and Fermions arranged into the Standard Model is more evidence of Intelligent Design.

The arranging of Hadrons as seen in the Baryon Octet, the Baryon Decuplet and the Meson Nonet further demonstrates order in the universe.

One might ask, why does it matter?

If God is the chief architect that designed the universe, then I want to give credit, where credit is due. Or as the scriptures say:

"Have ye not known? Have ye not heard? Hath it not been told you from the beginning? Have ye not understood from the foundations of the earth? It is He that sitteth upon the circle of the earth...that stretcheth out the heavens as a curtain and spreadth them out as a tent to dwell in." —Isaiah 40:21-22

In the above scripture, not only does it say that God stretched forth the known Universe, but also volunteers that the earth was circular hundreds of years before Pythagoras considered that since the moon was round that perhaps so was the earth.

"He stretcheth out the north over the empty place and hangeth the earth on nothing." —Job 26:7

Intelligent Design?

A loose definition of physics is applied math. To me that implies that there must be order to the universe.

What evidence do we see that demonstrates that the universe was designed and did not come about by mere chance?

Is it coincidence that all matter is comprised of triplets of quarks or could it be an indicator that the Trinity made their trade mark on the subatomic? Let's take a moment to consider…

On the cosmic scale

A moon or manmade satellite will orbit a planet in a circular path:

$$(x - h)^2 + (y - k)^2 = r^2$$

A planet will orbit a star in an elliptical path (Kepler's Laws):

$$\frac{(x-h)^2}{a^2} + \frac{(x-k)^2}{b^2} = r^2$$

A projectile launched from the surface of a planet follows a parabolic path:

$$(x - h)^2 = 4p(y - k)$$

Many comets orbit stars on hyperbolic paths:

$$\frac{(x-h)^2}{a^2} - \frac{(x-k)^2}{b^2} = r^2$$

Extra Material from the Author

The Higgs scalar field is able to impart mass to weak bosons of which the Z⁰ vector boson is illustrated possessing no charge and declaring it to Mr. Higgs (Z⁰ is neutral unlike the other Weak force carriers W+ and W-). Mr. Higgs is the scalar Higgs boson acting as a bank clerk, distributing 'masses' instead of money to his customers. Mass ratios of particles are displayed in place of the exchange rates for various currencies on a sign behind Mr. Higgs. It should be pointed out that 'mass' used here is not in the way that we might say, "a dumbbell weighs 30 Kg", but rather borrowing from Einstein's equation which relates matter and energy ($E=mc^2$), mass in the subatomic realm is expressed as the ratio of a particle's energy to the speed of light squared: $m=E/c^2$ [the units here are: $(GeV/m^2)/(s^2)$].

The next day as the brothers were returning by plane, Keith had a *déjà vu* experience. He felt as though he had been to Stockholm at an earlier date, or perhaps he had just dreamt it....

During the ceremony, Frank was allowed to speak. "Fellow scientists, in the way Kekulé was inspired by dreams, so my work has been a pursuit to understand a dream given to my brother Keith...." As everyone rose to their feet in applause, Keith was allowed to join Frank on the platform.

That autumn Keith got a call from Frank. "We're going to Sweden! I'm being awarded the Nobel Prize in Physics for discovering the <u>S</u>lepton <u>H</u>adronic <u>A</u>belian <u>R</u>eversal <u>K</u>aluza-Klein particle, or 'SHARK' particle, responsible for giving rise to the graviton."

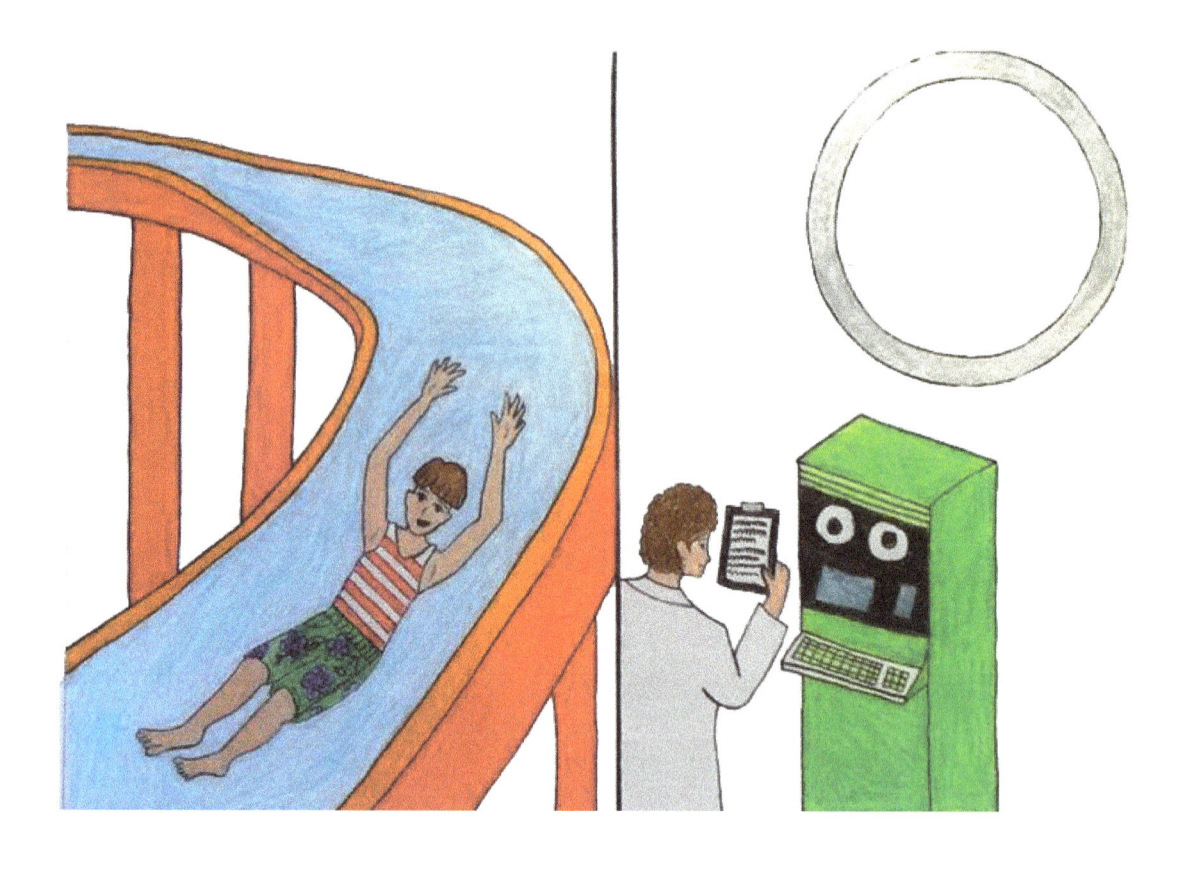

During the summer that followed, Frank stayed at the university and worked many late nights in the lab. Keith missed his brother but tried to enjoy summer vacation.

[26]The equations seen in this section are field equations from the Kaluza hypothesis, K-theory, M-theory and Kaluza-Klein geometry (i.e. $\Box\Phi$ is called the Massless Scalar equation). Kaluza and Klein expressed Einstein's field equations in five dimensions. In doing so, a theory arose which might unify electromagnetism with gravity. However, the pursuit for the graviton is still on!

$$\Box \Phi = \tfrac{1}{4} \Phi^3 F^{\alpha\beta} F_{\alpha\beta}$$

$$\Box \equiv g^{\mu\nu} \nabla_\mu \nabla_\nu$$

$$\tilde{\Gamma}^{\mu}_{55} = -\tfrac{1}{2} g^{\mu\alpha} \partial_\alpha \Phi^2.$$

Keith awoke in his bed to the sound of rain on his bedroom window. At breakfast Frank asked Keith about school, but Keith said, "I'd rather talk about the standard model." Frank said, "Have you been reading my textbooks again?" Keith told Frank all about his dream. Frank was astonished and spent the rest of the day at the library looking up journal articles and deriving **equations**[26].

[25] A neutrino is a lepton possessing both a 1/2 integer spin and very little mass. Neutrinos come in various flavors like quarks. Although they are governed by the weak nuclear force (on a small scale, seen in the beta decay of atomic nuclei), they do appear on the cosmic scale when a star goes supernova. Moreover, spinning neutron stars called pulsars exert extreme pressure on atomic nuclei forcing electrons into the nucleus where they react with protons and make neutrons. When this occurs, neutrinos are expelled.

Keith asked, "Can you get me home?" The gravitons replied, "We now possess the ability to cause your sub to be attracted to anything which possesses mass. In this case your house or bedroom." As they were flying Keith home, they passed through what seemed to be a colorful meteor storm. The gravitons told Keith it was just the Spring **Neutrino Showers**[25].

[24] Non-abelian means non-communitive as seen in the multiplication of matrices, the product of matrix A and B may not equal the product of matrix B and A. Quantum Chromodynamics is an example of a non-abelian gauge theory.

Suddenly, the cocoons broke open and three particles sprouted wings. They cried, "It's okay Keith we were the quarks (caterpillars) that were inside Sully! We have undergone a type of metamorphosis called the **non-abelian**[24] transmutation which transformed us into free floating gravitons."

[23] The word 'gauge' refers to gauge theory; it is a field theory in which the Lagrangian is invariant (a property of a system which remains unchanged) under a continuous group of local transformations. Some problems in field theory can be explained in terms of group theory.

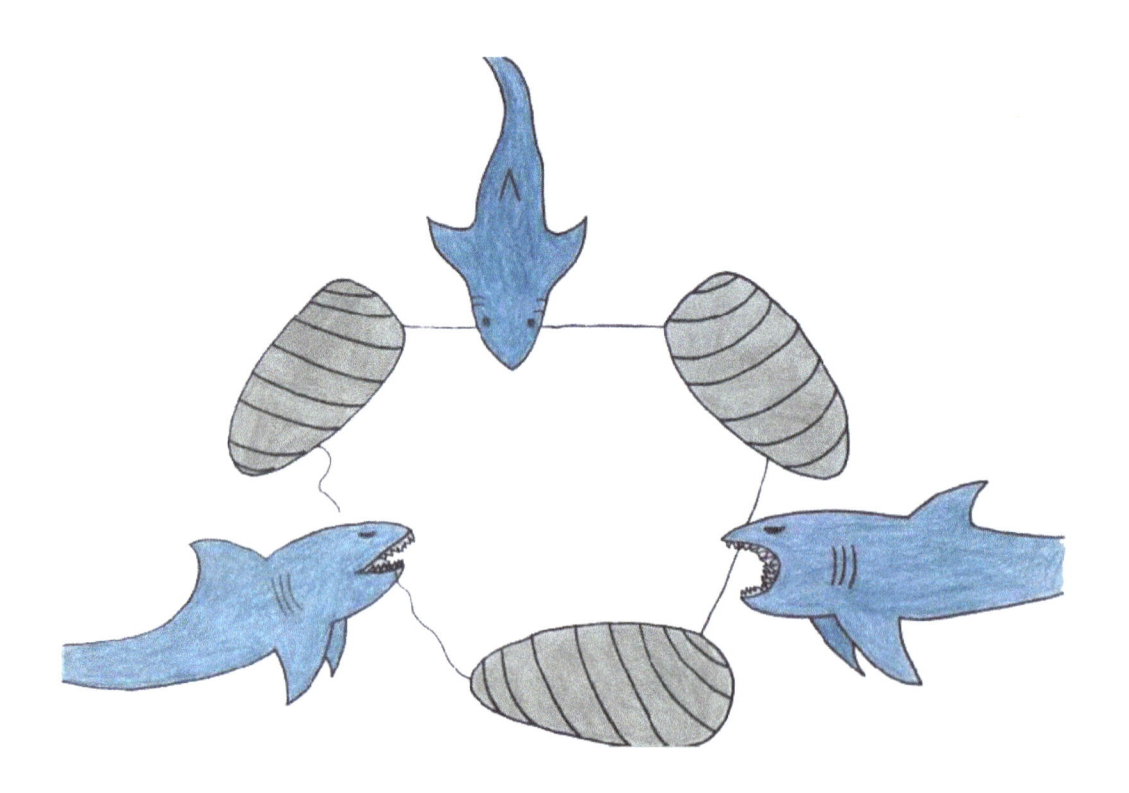

Keith was now aware that he had been dreaming and tried to wake himself up. It was no use, the trains struck and instantly it seemed like everything was under water. There were particles that looked like sharks swimming around his submarine. The 'sharks' began to gnaw at the cords that connected the three cocoons. When Keith first saw the particles chew through the strings, he couldn't **gauge**[23] exactly what was going on. The 'sharks' are mediators of the gravitational force. They release quarks from their confinement by changing them into gravitons.

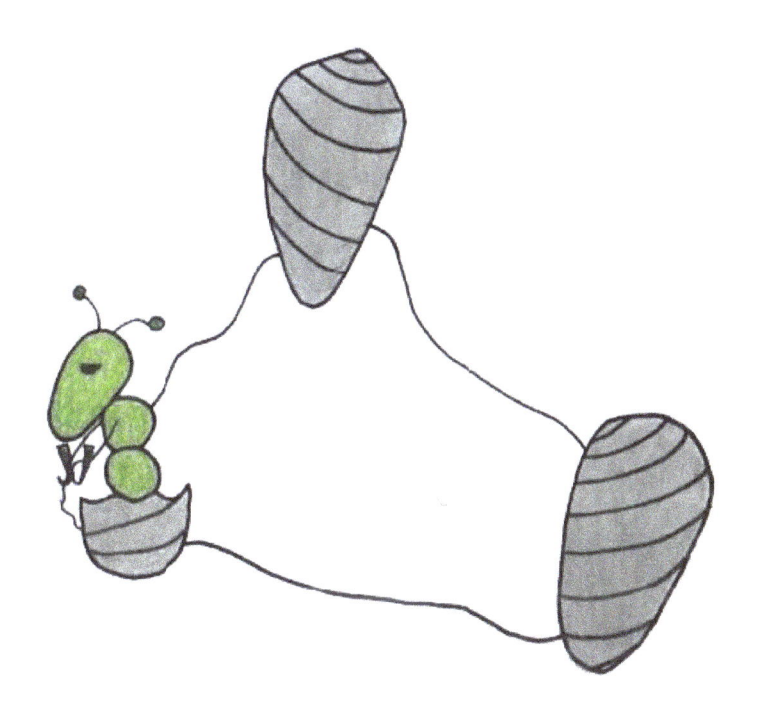

As Keith attempted to communicate with the quarks in Sully's heart, they said, "We'll see you on the other side kid!" They then spun cocoons around themselves. Sully said, "It's show time kid! Get inside me and stay in your submarine; something wonderful is about to happen!"

[22]In particle accelerators, particles and their anti-matter counter parts (here protons in the red train and anti-protons in the cyan train) are flung at each other in order to invoke annihilation. The particles are focused and accelerated via electromagnets. Annihilation gives rise to other particles, some of which may never have been previously observed.

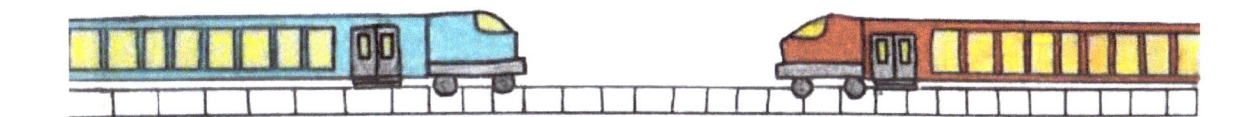

In no time at all, the train was accelerated to a rate that Keith had never dreamt of. It appeared that the train was on a **collision course**[22] with another train carrying passengers that looked like Harry (now a proton).

When the tank arrived at its destination, they saw particles boarding a train. Sully said, "Let's go kid. I've got connections, we're riding with the engineer!"

Fill With Antiprotons
Deliver to Synchrotron

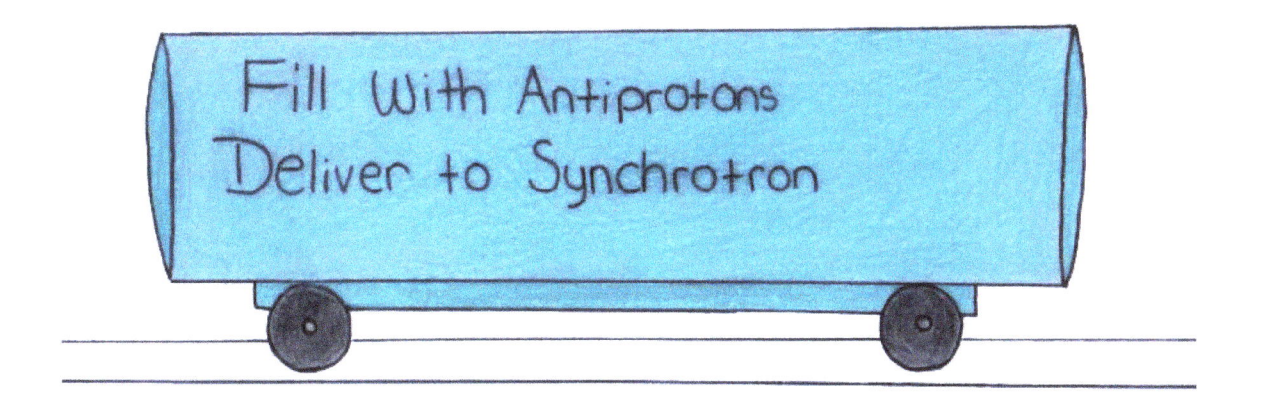

Sully said, "Hey kid, if you really want to go on an adventure, stowaway with me in this empty tank…."

[21]Melvin is an anti-neutron, he has the same ratio of up and down quarks as those in a neutron. However, since these are antiquarks, they possess anti-color charge. These are represented by the anti-colors of cyan (negative red), yellow (negative blue) and magenta (negative green). It is the gluon which mediates the changing of color charge amongst the quarks. There are eight different color combinations of gluons (known as the "color octet") which confine the quarks and conserve color charge. An anti-neutron can be formed when an anti-neutrino of the electron type (that possesses a threshold energy of 1.806 MeV) encounters a proton and yields both a neutron and a positron. This is known as inverse beta decay (or positron emission).

Sully volunteered that his cousin Melvin also was regarded as a black sheep (as they are each made of anti-matter). Sully said, "He shouldn't beat himself up, he has a good heart." Sully then showed Keith a picture of Melvin's heart (as he was a <u>type</u> of neutron being comprised of an anti-up quark and two anti-down quarks), Keith was awed by the very **bizarre colors**[21]

Keith stepped out of the Café to collect his thoughts when he was approached by a shady looking particle. Keith said, "Are you also related to Harry Baryon?" The particle replied, "They call me the black sheep of the family, I go by Sully."

[20] Since Eta-C is comprised of matter and anti-matter of the same mass, a reaction can take place mediated by the strong force (hence, 'gluon cocktail'). The meson states π+, K⁰ and K⁻ are the products of the reaction.

Harry said, "The Mayor is a great guy! As long as you keep him away from a gluon cocktail, else like Jekyll and Hyde, he seems to have a **split**[20] personality."

[19] Mesons are particles comprised of only two quarks. Eta-c is a meson comprised both of a Charm quark and an anti-Charm quark; hence they are mirror images of each other.

Harry introduced Keith to the Mayor 'Eta-C'. He was full of charm! When Harry peered into his heart, he saw a quark starring at itself in a **mirror**[19].

[18] The Omega-minus (Ω-) particle is comprised of 3 strange quarks.

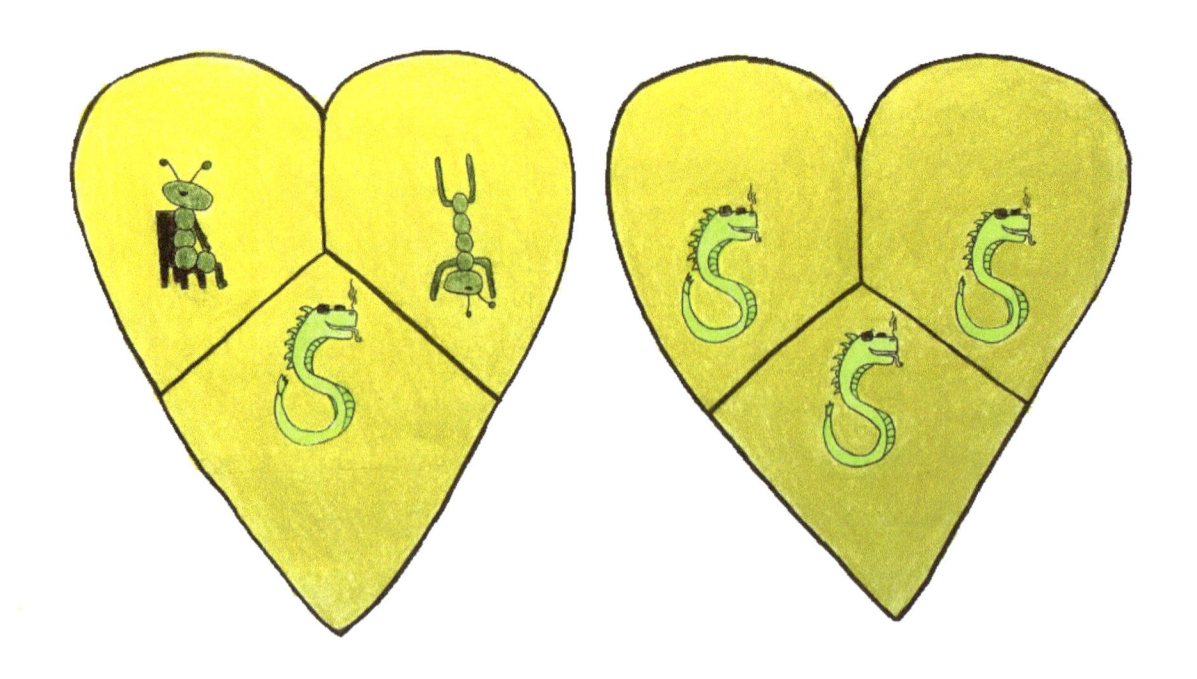

Keith found that he could understand a particle's character by looking into its heart. Lambda seemed a little strange, but **Omega Minus was strange through and through**[18].

[17] A Lambda (Λ) particle is a baryon comprised of the following 3 quarks: up, down, and strange (depicted by a serpent in the next illustration).

Harry said, "Meet a couple other baryons. They are cousins of mine, **Lambda**[17] and Omega Minus."

[14] In the above scenario Harry's 'change of heart' is the conversion of a neutron into a proton. This transformation is thought to be mediated by a **W-boson** [hence 'Big Boson' is overseeing the Café]. A boson is a carrier of the weak nuclear force.

[15] A helium atom is comprised of 2 protons, 2 neutrons and 2 electrons. When the caterpillar flips, Harry becomes a proton like Sally (two protons). The new horn player joins the bass player to make two neutrons. Lastly, two electrons were added to the payroll.

[16] The conversion of a neutron to a proton previously mentioned gives rise to both an electron and an anti-neutrino of the electron type. Notice that they are not on the payroll (as they do not comprise the helium atom; they are investors in the Helium Café). The electron and anti-neutrino are byproducts of this subatomic reaction known as beta decay.

The head of the Café's board of directors, known as **'Big Boson**[14]**'** decided to restructure. Henry had a change of heart and now sang duets with Sally; a new neutral horn player was hired. The Café under new supervision was renamed **Helium**[15] Café. Two investors, James the electron and Ronny the **anti-neutrino of the electron type**[16] were present to witness the business refinance. Everyone got a raise and one of the caterpillars formerly in a headstand was paid a bonus to now sit upright. Two electrons were also added to the payroll and lit up the Café for the grand opening.

[11]Although the colored force fields can switch amongst the caterpillars, all three colors must be present to conserve what is known as 'color charge'. In reality there are no colored quarks. The term 'color' is used by physicists to distinguish the parameter of color charge from that of electric charge.

[12]Nuclear color charge exhibits lines of force between quarks in the same way that one can observe flux lines between the North and South poles of a bar magnet using iron files.

[13]Just as the photon is the force carrier or mediator of the electromagnetic force between charged particles, so the gluon is the force carrier of the strong force. However, unlike charged particles which obey the Inverse Square Law, when two quarks try to move apart, the strong force drives them back together with an intensity proportional to the squared (not inversely squared) distance by which the quarks moved apart. This is accomplished via gluons creating a confinement field which we see here as the aura of Harry's golden heart.

Suddenly the field surrounding the caterpillar in the chair switched colors with the field around one of the down quarks. Keith asked, "What just happened and why are you guys linked together by what appears to be telephone cords?" The caterpillar replied, "Let's just say it is a way of **conserving**[11] energy around here. What you referred to as 'cords' are **color flux lines**[12] that keep us connected, but only Harry's golden heart keeps us in this room (<u>**a gluon field of confinement**</u>[13]). It was a fluctuation of the gluon field that made us change colors a minute ago."

[10]Any particle comprised of 3 quarks is called a Baryon. A neutron is comprised of 2 down quarks and an up quark whereas a proton has 2 up quarks and a down quark. Each of the 3 quarks in each of these scenarios has a different 'color charge' (as seen in the next illustration), displayed as blue, green and red force fields which enshroud the caterpillars. If one of the down quarks (represented by the caterpillars in headstands) in the neutron were to become an up quark, the neutron would become a proton (a proton possessing a <u>positive</u> charge).

Keith introduced himself to a caterpillar in a chair and asked why the other two were in headstands. The insect sitting upright explained that they were down quarks and that he was an up quark. He also commented that if one of those guys in a headstand were to flip over, it would make for a more **positive**[10] atmosphere.

Harry continued, "If you can further shrink your submarine, you're welcome to come in and see more." Keith pressed the shrink button and made his way into Harry's heart.

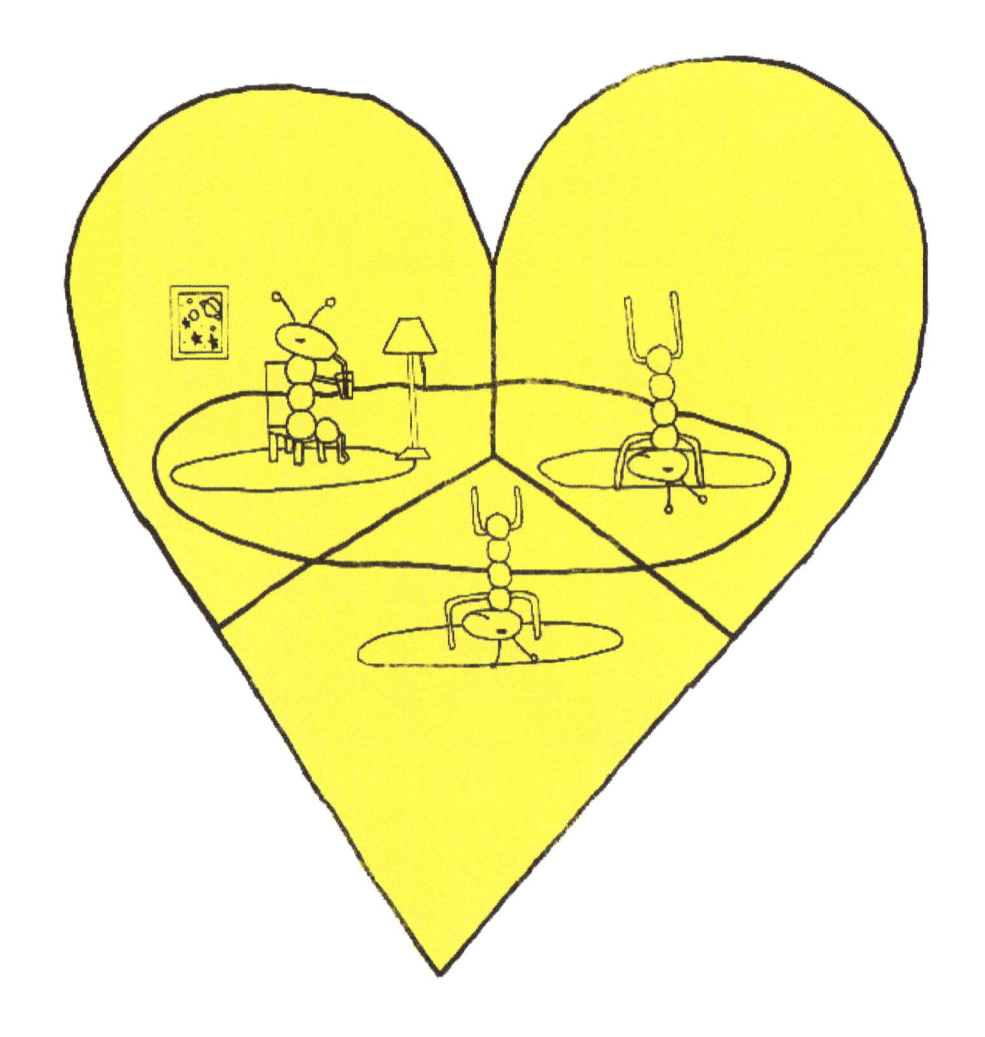

After Harry's trumpet solo, he turned to Keith and said, "Hi, I'm Harry Baryon. Come here, I want you to see what's at the heart of things around here." When Harry got close enough, Keith could see into Harry as though he were peering through tinted glass.

[8]The mass of a neutron is almost identical to that of a proton yet the neutron possesses no charge.

[9]When Harry the Neutron joins the group, there are now one proton (Sally) and two neutrons (the bass and trumpet players); this is indicative of a Tritium nucleus (one more neutron than that of deuterium).

Just as Keith was finishing his drink, the bass player (a neutron) said, "Hey kid, get ready, Harry's about to join us on the horn! He's another laid back, **neutral**[8] kind of guy like me. Dude, things are going to get so heavy in here they'll want to change the name of the café to **Tritium**[9]."

[4]We are told on the next page that the bass player is a neutron; since the vocalist is a proton, the Café is indicative of a deuterium nucleus. A normal Hydrogen nucleus contains only a proton and no neutron(s).

[5]Protons have a positive charge equal and opposite to that of an electron (that's why the electrons in the audience are attracted to the singer who is a proton).

[6]Electrons that orbit the nucleus of an atom are attracted to the protons in the nucleus.

[7]The reason why the electrons do not collapse into the nucleus to meet the protons there is because the electrons' momenta allow them to maintain orbits much like satellites orbiting the Earth (the orbits do not decay because the satellites possess enough momenta to satisfy Newton's Law of Inertia).

Keith grew thirsty so he walked to the **Deuterium**[4] Café. He heard a female vocalist and male accompaniment on bass guitar. The base player said to Keith, "Isn't she great? She has such a **positive**[5] attitude that everyone around here is **attracted**[6] to her but they can't slow down[7] enough in their busy schedules to get to know her."

9

[1] In molecular orbital theory, electrons that become promoted to higher energy levels are said to be, "excited".

[2] The Heisenberg <u>Uncertainty</u> Principle tells us that we cannot know both the momentum and the position of an electron in space.

[3] The Pauli Exclusion Principle tells us if two electrons occupy the same orbital they are paired with <u>opposite spin</u>.

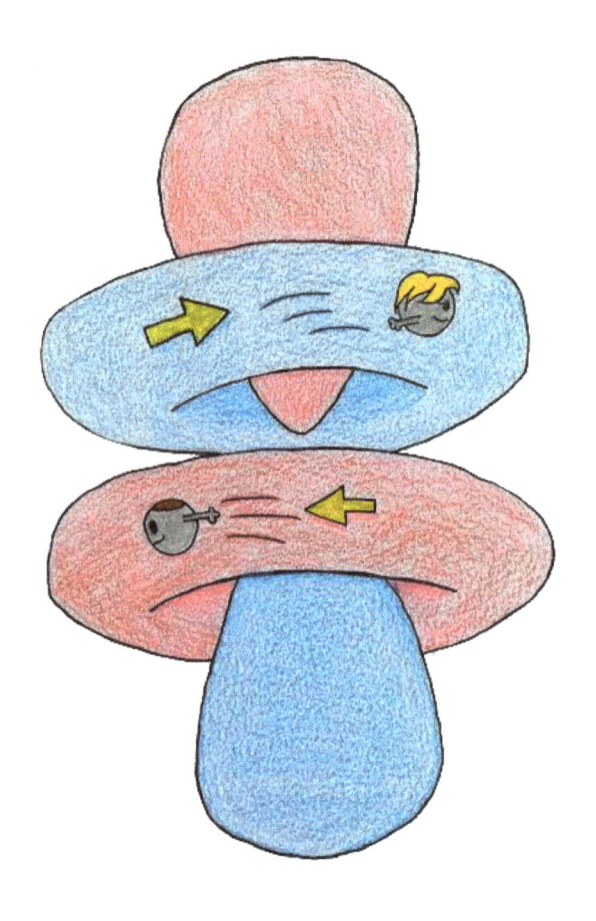

As he passed through layers of electrons, some of which appeared to be **excited**[1], he asked where they were headed. A pair of electrons who appeared to be dancing from a distance replied, "The answer to your question has a degree of **uncertainty**[2]." Keith asked one of the electrons why his friend was on a different floor of the transparent dance studio. The electron replied, "Because she is <u>**spinning the other direction**</u>[3]!"

Keith dreamt that he was the pilot of a submarine navigating the dimensions of the subatomic realm.

After Frank left, Keith realized that Frank left his book on the shelf in Keith's room. Although it was "lights out", Keith often read by moonlight. Since it was Spring Break, he was not worried about waking up early for school. Keith fell asleep while reading about quantum chromodynamics.

That night Frank came to tuck in Keith. "Mom and Dad said you won the science fair this year, good job sport! It's nice to be home, see you at breakfast."

Keith was excited to see Frank and hear about the things he was learning in school.

Keith's brother Frank was returning from college on Spring Break.

There was a young boy named Keith who was a dreamer.

PREFACE

The author suggests that the book be first read as a story, an allegory of subatomic physics. If the reader then chooses to delve deeper, they should reread while referencing the foot notes which expound on the topics being presented.

ACKNOWLEDGEMENTS

Thank you to my wife and children for all playing a part in this project in some fashion whether it be in the preparation of the book or the marketing of it.

Thank you for all of your prayers and support!

Gotham Books

30 N Gould St.
Ste. 20820, Sheridan, WY 82801
https://gothambooksinc.com/

Phone: 1 (307) 464-7800

© 2024 *Danny R. Martineau Jr.* All rights reserved.

No part of this book may be reproduced, stored in a retrieval system, or transmitted by any means without the written permission of the author.

Published by Gotham Books (July 4, 2024)

ISBN: 979-8-88775-925-8 (P)
ISBN: 979-8-88775-926-5 (E)

Because of the dynamic nature of the Internet, any web addresses or links contained in this book may have changed since publication and may no longer be valid.

The views expressed in this work are solely those of the author and do not necessarily reflect the views of the publisher, and the publisher hereby disclaims any responsibility for them.

QUARKS & SHARKS

Written by Danny R. Martineau Jr.

Illustrations by Isabella S. Martineau

Color Enhancement by Andrew Z. Martineau

QUARKS & SHARKS

$$S(\hat{g}) = \Lambda \int_m \{R(g) - \frac{1}{\Lambda}|F|^2\}vol(g)$$